Love my Native Hair

WHY SO SPECIAL

By

SOPHIA JASO & RICHARD JASO

Dedication

For all of the missing native women who helped inspire on spreading the native word.

About the Author

My Father and I are proud Yaqui Natives and we are proud of our culture. We feel Natives are a topic not often discussed and we want to help shed some light on this but in a fun and special way. Welcome to our Native Journey.

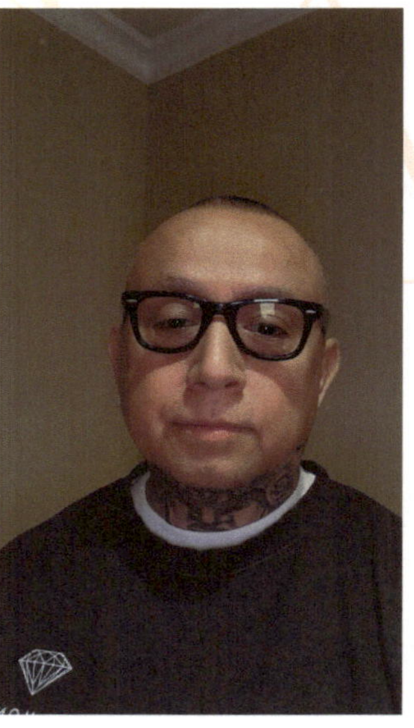

Acknowledgement

I would like to thank my Jaso Family and all fellow Natives.

Hi my name is Lomasi, which means
"Pretty Flower"

Hi my name is Takoda, which means
"friend to everyone"

Lomasi and I we will be your guide for
this story.

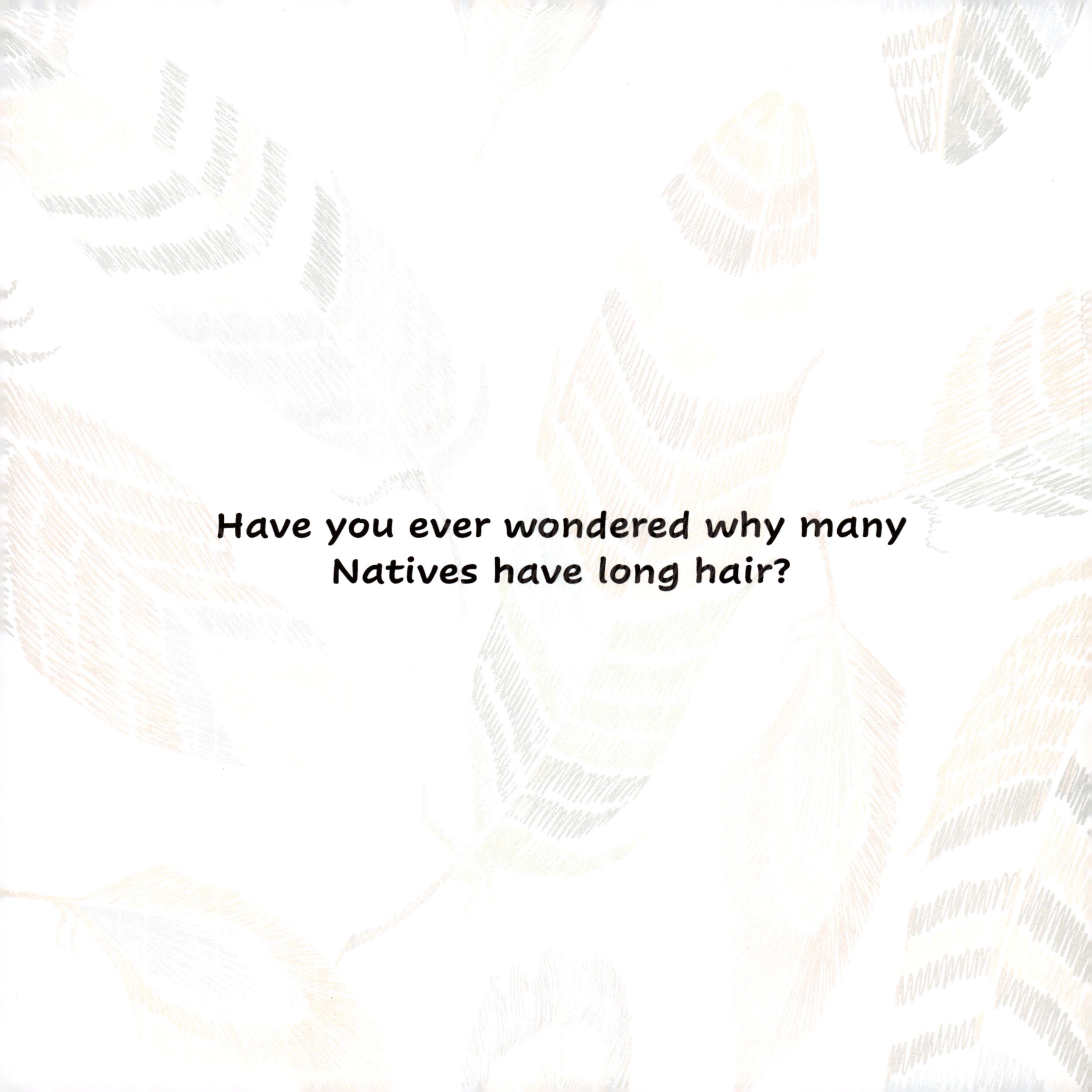

Have you ever wondered why many
Natives have long hair?

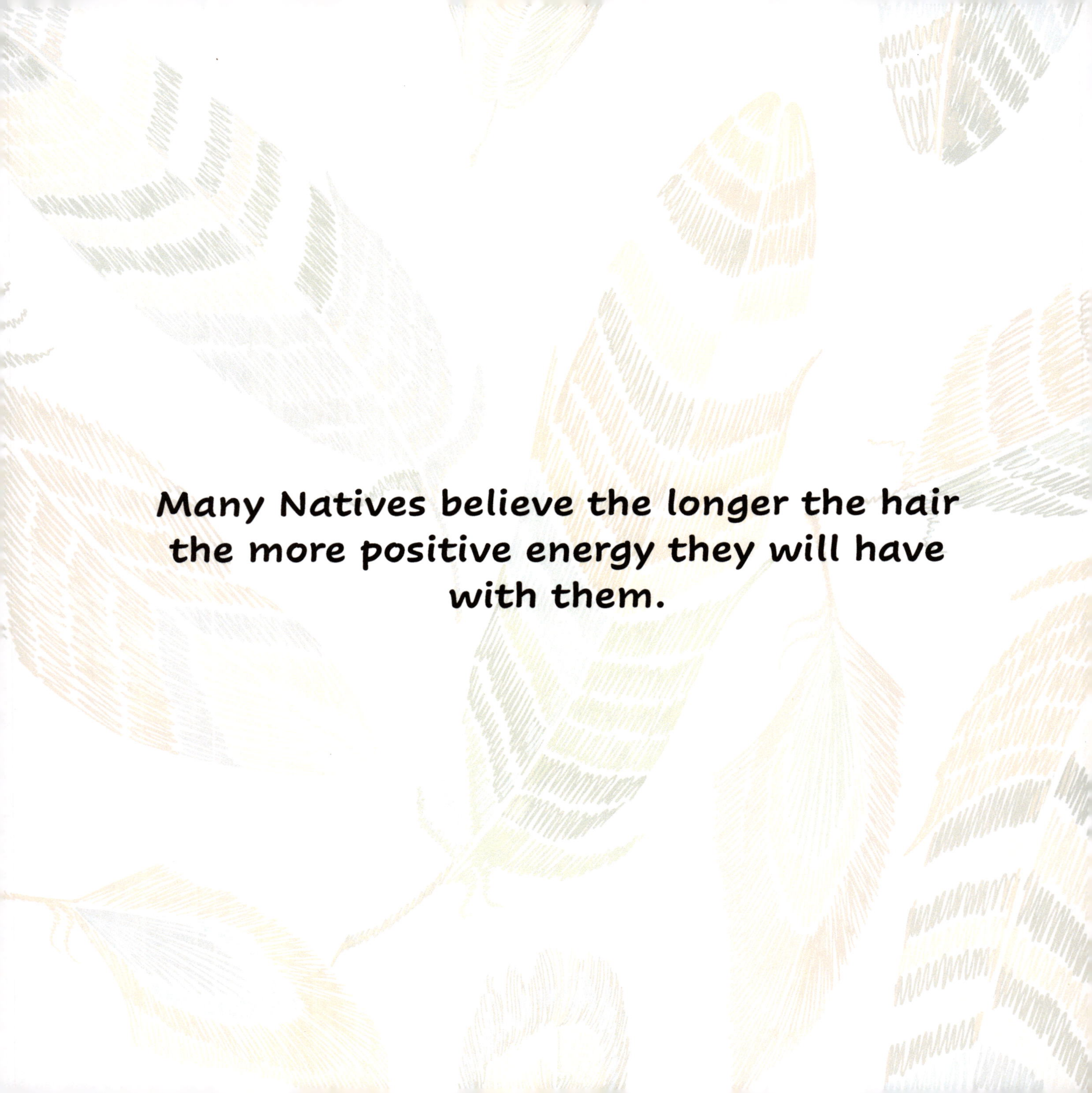

Many Natives believe the longer the hair the more positive energy they will have with them.

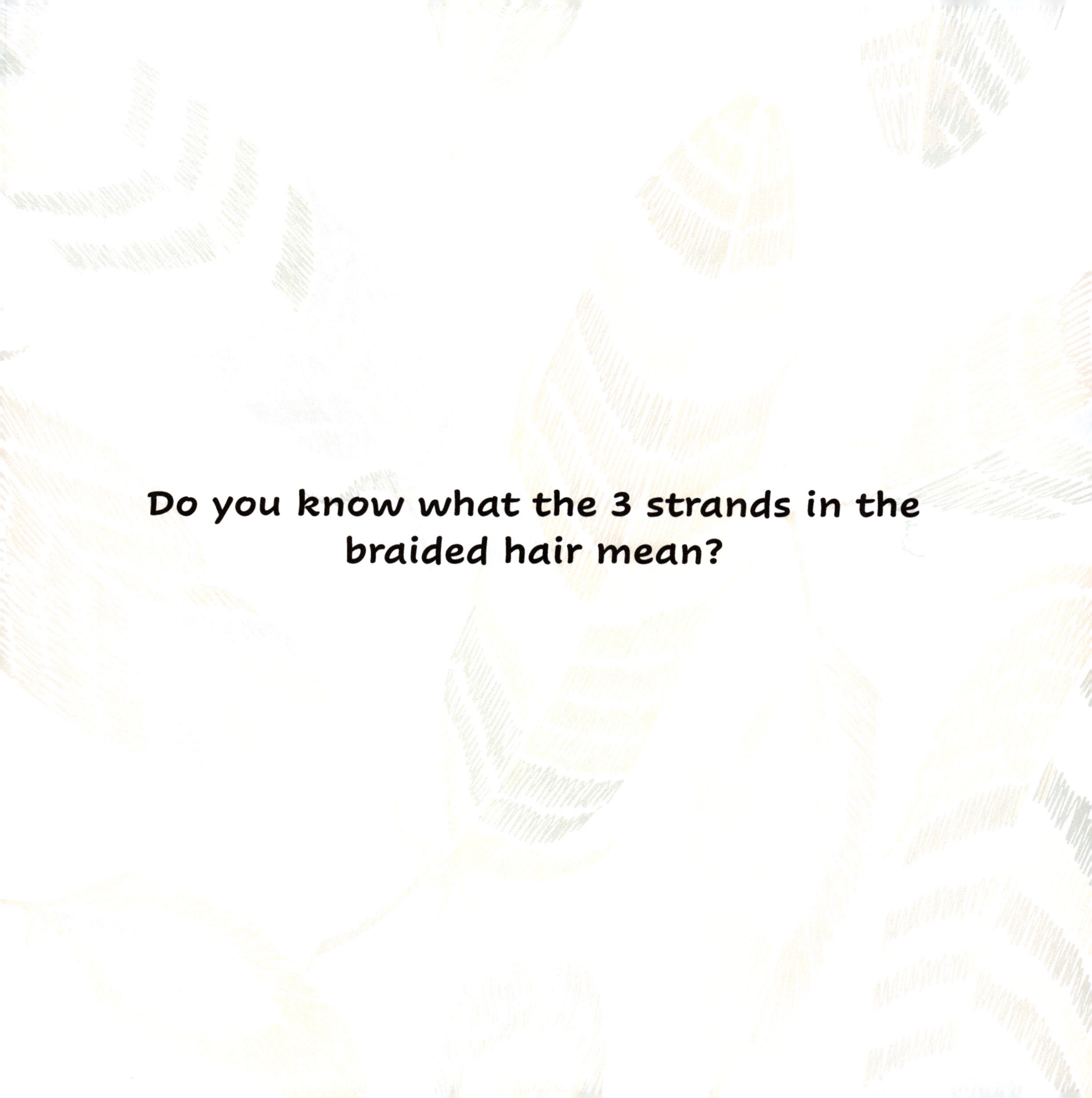

Do you know what the 3 strands in the braided hair mean?

Mind
Body
Spirit

Do Natives cut their hair?

Yes, they do.
Some do not cut their hair ever and some do often.
Would you like to know why some do?

Well, if this is their first time ever cutting their hair.....

A ceremony happens!!!

Some cut their hair when someone they
love passes away

All hair cuts are treated with love and care

Sometimes the hair that was cut is
buried out of respect.

Do you know who can touch our hair?

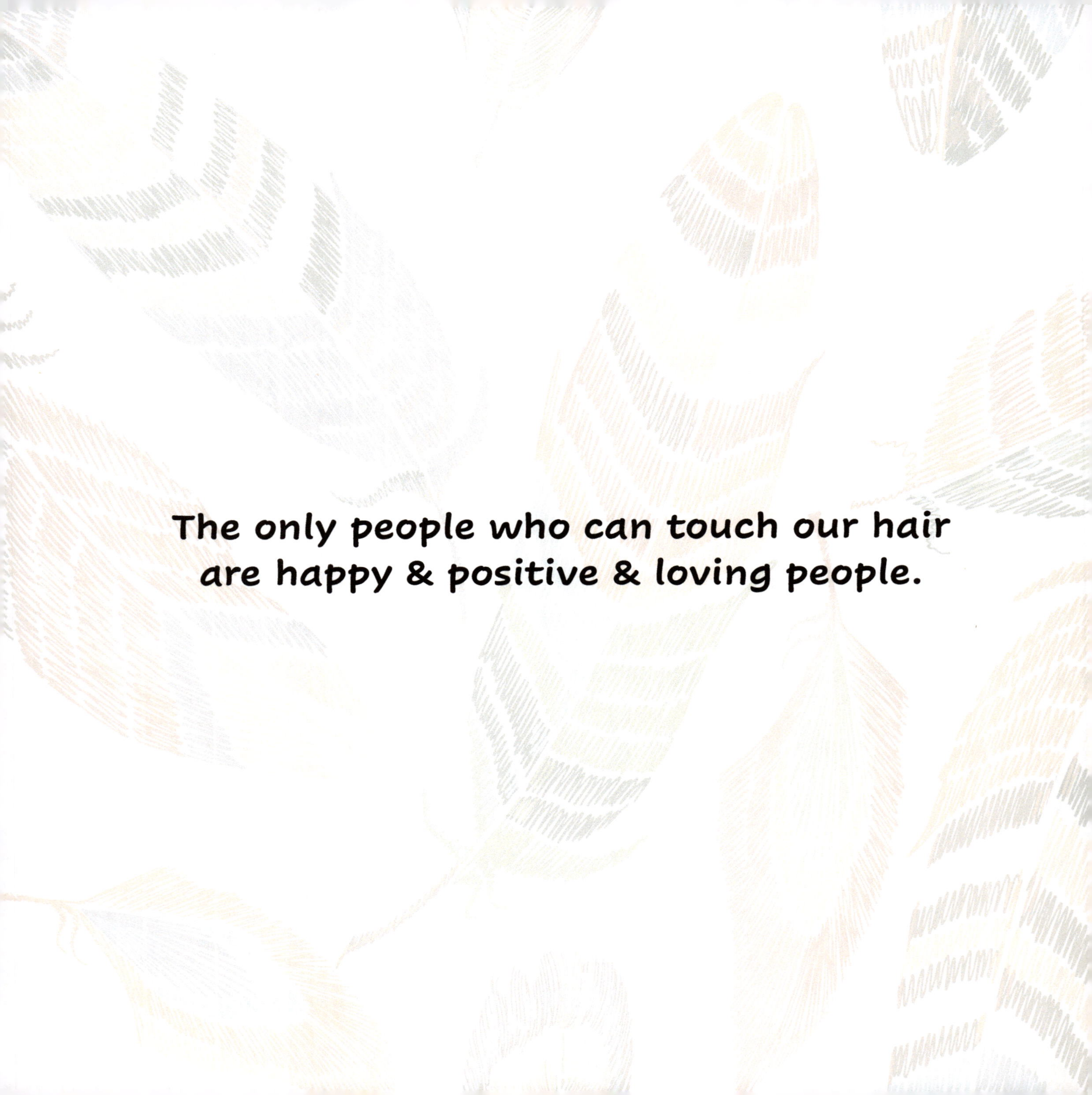
The only people who can touch our hair
are happy & positive & loving people.

Those who touch our hair pass on that
love and happiness to us.

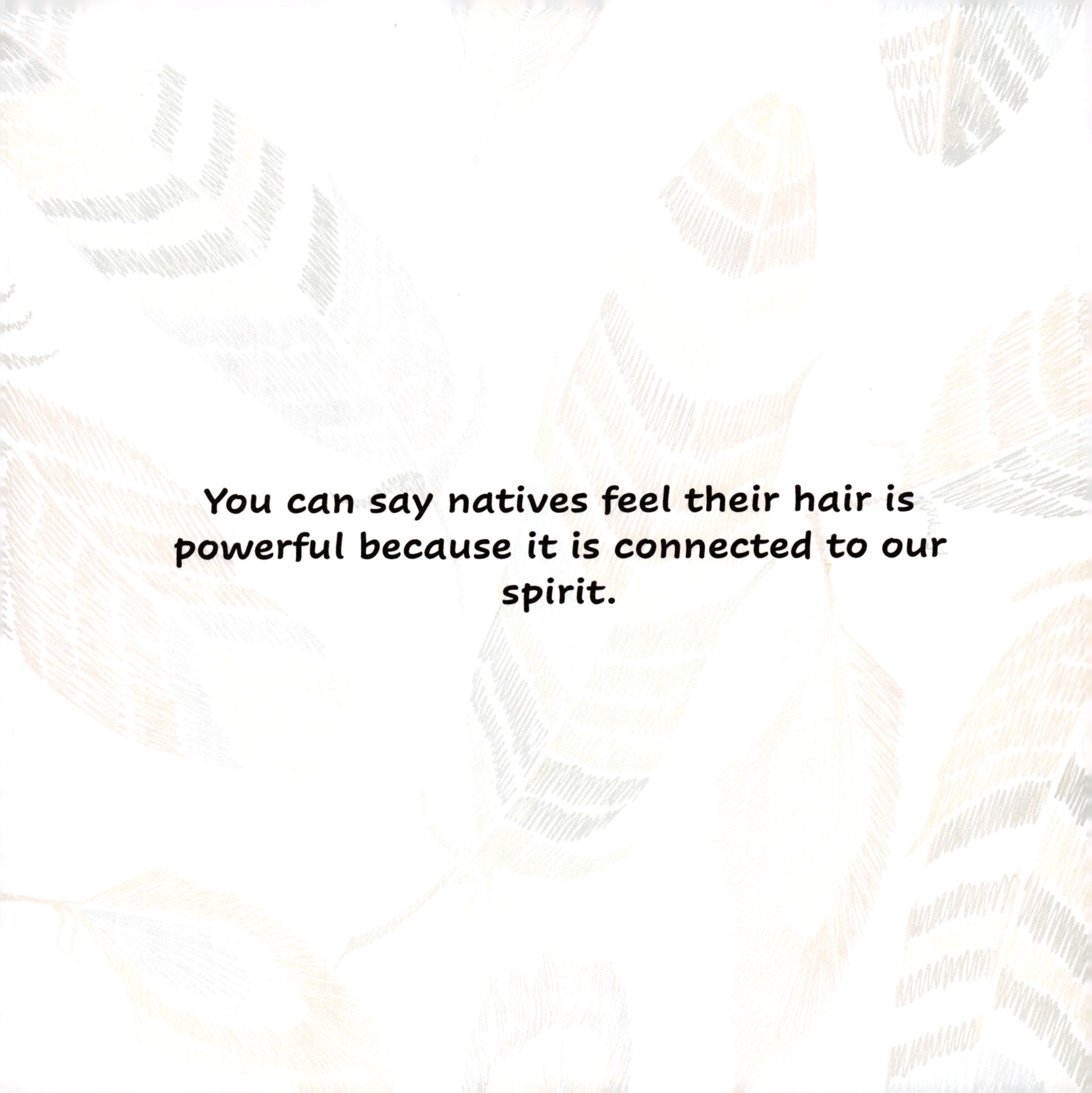
You can say natives feel their hair is powerful because it is connected to our spirit.

Do you want to know something else.....

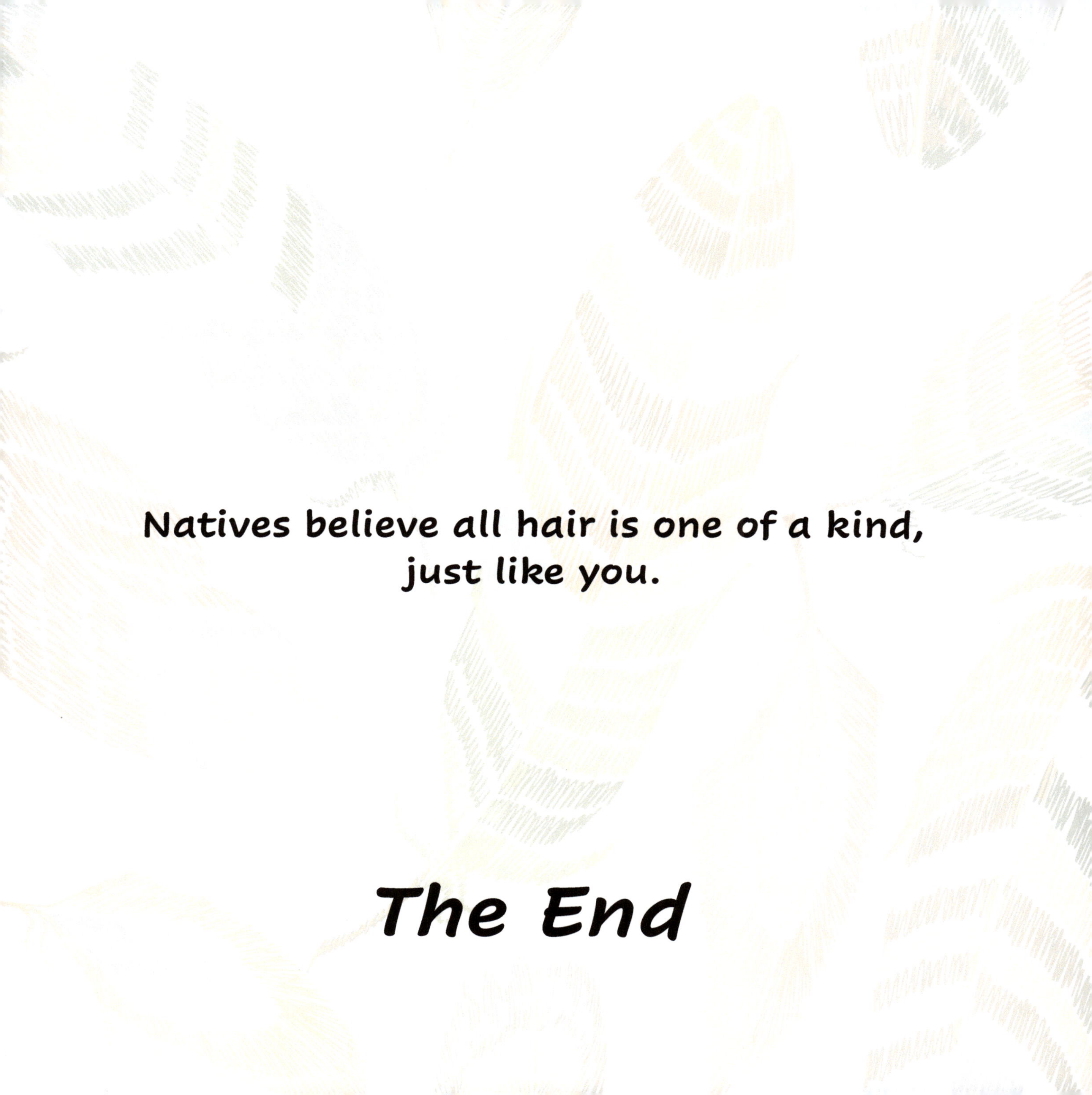

Natives believe all hair is one of a kind,
just like you.

The End